Breathe, Sis!

Breathe, Sis!

This is just a chapter;
it's not your whole story.

Menzaire Boykins-Esters

tucker
publishing house llc

Publishing Services provided by Tucker Publishing House, LLC
10100 W. McNichols Rd Suite 323
Detroit, MI 48221
www.tuckerpublishinghouse.com

Book Menzaire to speak at your next event:
authorm.boykinsesters@gmail.com

Table of Contents

Introduction

Life can change in an instant. One moment, everything feels normal, and the next, you're standing at the edge of an unimaginable storm. I know this because it happened to me. At 39 years old, I suffered a hemorrhagic stroke caused by an undiagnosed arteriovenous malformation (AVM)—a condition I never knew I had until it nearly took my life. I had no prior symptoms, no warnings. The only sign was a slight tightness in my neck, something I had attributed to a previous car accident. But inside my body, a silent threat had been there since birth, waiting for the right moment to rupture.

I went to sleep three times before seeking medical attention, completely unaware that I was in the middle of a life-threatening emergency. Medical experts say that stroke patients should receive treatment within three hours of their first symptoms, yet I slept for at least eight hours before heading to the hospital. By all accounts, I should not be here. But by the grace of God, I am.

This book is not just my story—it is my testimony. A testimony of faith, healing, and purpose. I am sharing it because I am being obedient to the Lord. He carried me through my darkest hours and spared my life so that I could bring awareness, inspire, and educate others. Stroke recovery is long and difficult—not just for the survivor but for their loved ones as well. The after-effects can be devastating, both physically and emotionally. I lost the ability to write and talk, my vision was impaired, and my body felt foreign to me. But through it all, God's mercy sustained me.

Today, I am a walking miracle. I was discharged with no medication, and I am still not on any medication to this day. My body has been fully restored, and my spirit has been completely transformed. Before my stroke, I was quiet, reserved, and hesitant to express my feelings. I kept things bottled up. Now, I am bold, vocal, and unapologetic about my truth. I no longer waste time on relationships that drain me or environments that don't serve me. I have learned to set boundaries, prioritize my well-being, and live with intention and purpose.

Through my journey, I've also gained a deep compassion for stroke survivors and caregivers.

The lack of knowledge I had before my stroke has fueled my passion to educate others on the warning signs and symptoms of stroke—especially within the African American community, where health disparities often lead to delayed diagnoses and worse outcomes. I want other women—especially Black women—to understand the importance of advocating for their health, listening to their bodies, and trusting God even in the darkest moments.

My life is completely different now, but I wouldn't change a thing. I see the world differently. I cherish every moment. God removed people from my life who weren't meant to go with me into my next season, and though that pruning was painful, it was necessary for my growth. He sent me women of substance, a tribe that truly supports and uplifts me. Through it all, He taught me the greatest lesson of all—put your trust in Him, not in man.

As you read this book, I pray that my journey encourages you, whether you are recovering from a stroke, supporting a loved one, or simply navigating one of life's unexpected storms. This is more than a memoir; this is a guide to faith, healing, and resilience.

Whatever you are facing right now, *Breathe, Sis*— this is just a chapter, not your whole story. God is still writing the rest.

Menzaire Boykins-Esters

CHAPTER 1

Today, I CHOOSE Life

Self-Care Tip Box: *Start the day with intention, prayer, and embracing the power of choice.*

Quote: "In life, you have three choices. Give up, give in, or give it your all" – Charleston Parker.

Scripture Reading: "Whatever you ask in prayer, believe that you have received it, and it will be yours" (Mark 11:24, NIV).

My Story: We often face choices that define our paths in our life's journey. These decisions shape our experiences, mold our character, and ultimately determine our destiny. One choice that is particularly significant is living intentionally, purposefully, and without fear. This decision requires courage, conviction, and faith. It's a commitment to opportunities, a wise selection of companions, and trust in the divine report of the Lord.

In Isaiah 53:5, the Bible declares, "And with his stripes, we are **HEALED**." This powerful statement served as comfort, hope, and a testament to God's healing power during my valley experience. I align myself with this divine promise by believing and speaking victory over every situation. I position myself to receive miracles, expecting Jehovah Rapha, the Lord who heals, to make a way where there seems to be no way.

Because I **CHOOSE** to live intentionally, I stand as a walking miracle, a living testimony of God's healing power. I recognize that life can change in the blink of an eye, and I understand the importance of living a purposeful life. I have learned to value each moment, each breath, and each opportunity that comes my way.

Choosing to live intentionally is not always easy. It requires us to step out of our comfort zones, confront our fears, and face uncertainties. In these moments of challenges, we grow, evolve, become stronger, and indeed come alive.

Before my stroke, I had a life of health and vitality. Each day after work, I began with a brisk three-mile walk, a ritual invigorating my body and preparing my mind for a good night's rest. My commitment to wellness extended beyond personal habits; it was a foundation of my identity as a member of Brightmoor Christian Church. For over 21 years, I've dedicated myself to serving others as a General Motors (GM) customer support specialist. This is where I gained excellent communication skills, strong problem-solving skills, automotive knowledge, relationship-building skills, patience, and empathy.

My passion for promoting health and well-being flourished through Divine Juicing, my side business that was more than just a venture—it was a **mission**. Our slogan, "Inspire humanity to ingest healthy, organic, and fruitful divine juice that feeds the mind, body, and soul," was not merely a catchy phrase but a reflection of my life's purpose. Advocating for healthy living, having a voice in the community, and guiding others toward nourishment and care, is a way of life for me.

I started Divine Juicing in the spring of 2020, during the height of the COVID-19 pandemic. Inspired by Tony Robbins' book, "Money Master the Game," I discovered a profound love for juicing and the realization that true wealth comes from serving others. The journey of Divine Juicing began long before the company's inception, with a simple act of love—preparing nourishing juices for my husband. As the pandemic unfolded, I realized I could help because this virus affected my family and friends' immune systems. With a heart set on contributing value and service, I started crafting immune-boosting ginger shots. This small gesture of care quickly blossomed into a thriving business, profiting over $7,000 within three months. I was pleasantly surprised. I didn't know what to expect, but it wasn't that!

God is so purposeful in all that He does. I was unaware that the storm was approaching, but He wasn't. The Lord prepared for the brand promise. "Let's Stay Healthy Together," which encapsulates the essence of Divine Juicing. He prepared me before I knew I was being prepared. God cares about humanity, and this call was a call to action, a shared commitment to well-being, and a reminder that health is a collective pursuit. I was honored to be a part of this healthy movement. Things were going well, and I was excited for the future.

Life quickly took a turn. At 39, in what I believed to be the prime of my life, my world was turned upside down. The stroke came without warning, like a thief in the night stealing away the certainties I had built my life upon. In those moments of vulnerability, when my physical strength halted, I confronted a profound truth: I had been going through the motions without truly grasping the depth of my existence.

The recovery journey was vigorous, marked by moments of despair and frustration. Yet, within this test of faith and transformation, I discovered a resilience I never knew I possessed. The stroke, while an agonizing experience, became a catalyst for significant personal growth. It taught me to slow down, appreciate life's fragility, and understand that every breath is a gift not to be squandered.

As I navigated the complexities of rehabilitation, my perspective on what it means to live one's best life evolved. No longer was it defined by the miles walked or the success of my business endeavors. Instead, it became about the connections established with family and friends, the compassion shared with strangers, and the inner peace cultivated through adversity.

Today, I stand not as a victim of circumstance but as a testament to God's miraculous healing power. The Divine Juicing mission, inspired by a deeper significance, still operates. We continue to inspire but with a renewed emphasis on cherishing each moment and recognizing the beauty in overcoming obstacles.

Honestly, my stroke did not signify an end but a beginning—a second chance to embrace life with open arms and a heart full of gratitude. It has been a humbling reminder that true health encompasses the physical, emotional, and spiritual realms. As I share my story, I hope to ignite a spark in others, encouraging them to live authentically and find joy in the journey, no matter how unexpected their paths are.

The Worst Headache

It was an evening like any other when my husband, Duawne, and I decided to unwind at a local lounge with a friend. The ambiance was inviting, the company was pleasant, and the night promised relaxation after a long week. However, as we approached the entrance and I reached for my identification, an unexpected and overwhelming pain surged through my head. The pain wasn't just a regular headache; it was a crippling sensation that seemed to surpass all others I had experienced before.

The intensity of the pain was alarming, and I couldn't help but express my distress to Duawne. "OMG, my head is hurting so bad." His immediate response was one of concern, coupled with the hope that some food and rest might alleviate the sudden discomfort. Yet, as we settled in and the food arrived, it became apparent that this was no ordinary headache. The pain persisted, unrelenting and fierce, and I was unable to eat the meal before me.

Duawne's instincts told him that something was seriously wrong. Heeding the severity of my symptoms, he suggested we abandon our plans and return home. The decision likely played a crucial role in what unfolded next. As we later learned, such intense headaches can be a warning of critical health issues, including the possibility of an aneurysm or other life-threatening conditions.

This experience was a striking reminder of the importance of listening to our bodies and not dismissing potential warning signs. It underscored the value of having a supportive husband who can act swiftly in moments of crisis. While the cause of the headache remained unknown at the time, the episode highlighted the need for prompt medical attention when faced with severe and inexplicable symptoms.

Take heed: my encounter with "the worst headache of my life" was a big ordeal that brought to light the fragility of health and the unpredictability of medical emergencies. It taught us the significance of vigilance and the power of timely intervention. As we navigate life, we need to remember to be attuned to our well-being and to advocate for our health, for it is often in these critical moments that our lives can change dramatically.

The night had taken an unforeseen and terrifying turn. As we left the lounge, my condition deteriorated rapidly. The world around me became a blur, and darkness enveloped my sight for a brief but eternal span of ten seconds. Panic surged through me as I began to vomit uncontrollably, the fear noticeable in my voice as I cried out to Duawne, "Help me, I can't see." My memory of that walk to the car is fragmented, overshadowed by the overwhelming need to lie down, to escape into sleep.

Duawne, forever my rock, grabbed my hand and guided me to the vehicle. I reclined the seat, trying to steady my spinning world while he urgently drove us home. The night air rushed through the car as if echoing my own turmoil. My mind was a whirlwind of dread and perplexity, struggling to make sense of what was happening to my body.

Upon reaching our driveway, a new symptom emerged—a tingling sensation crawling up my legs, robbing them of their strength. It was then I realized I could not walk. With a desperate attempt, I told Duawne, "Let me kick my shoes off so I can crawl up the stairs and into bed." The thought of crawling seemed more bearable than confronting the reality that my body was failing me.

With Duawne's support, I staggered towards the entrance of our home. Each step was a battle against the numbness spreading through my limbs. All I yearned for was the warmth of my bed, the comfort of sleep that I hoped would take away the nightmare of symptoms that had held me captive without warning.

In retrospect, this unbelievable experience was a critical wake-up call. It highlighted the importance of recognizing when symptoms may indicate a medical emergency. The sudden onset of a severe headache, vision loss, vomiting, and paralysis are all signs that necessitate immediate medical attention.

That night also taught me the invaluable lesson of never taking one's health for granted. It showed me the significance of acting swiftly in the face of alarming symptoms and the vital role loved ones play in times of crisis. It is a reminder to all of us to prioritize our health and well-being above all else, for in doing so, we may save our own lives.

It was a night like any other until it wasn't. The comfort of my bed and the warmth of sleep embraced me fully. But as the darkness of the room lingered, an unexpected awakening knocked me into consciousness. There I was, disoriented, my sense of balance betraying me at every attempt to stand. The world seemed to tilt and spin as I fought against the waves of nausea that threatened to overwhelm me.

Crawling became my only means of movement, yet even this early learned locomotion behavior proved challenging. My body, which had always been a vessel under my command, now felt foreign and unresponsive. The urge to reach the bathroom was strong, but my limbs conspired against me, leading me astray to the other bedroom.

The silence of the night was shattered by the sound of my body colliding with furniture—a loud BOOM that echoed through the house. Duawne's voice fell with concern, cutting through the haze of my confusion. "What is going on? Are you okay?" he asked, his words tinged with alarm.

My reply was a mixture of frustration and fear. "I was just trying to vomit in the toilet, but my body led me to the bedroom across the hall," I explained, the reality of my helplessness sinking in. "I don't know what's happening."

My movements were erratic and uncontrollable on the floor, reminiscent of a snake's slither. The struggle to gain mastery over my own form was surreal, leaving me with a profound sense of disbelief. As I attempted to position myself over the toilet, hoping to alleviate some discomfort, the hopelessness of the situation became painfully clear. It was in this moment of vulnerability that the truth dawned on me—something was deeply wrong.

This unsettling experience served as an absolute reminder of how quickly health can waver and the importance of seeking medical attention when our bodies signal distress. It underscored the delicacy of our well-being and the need to listen closely to what our physical selves are trying to communicate. In the end, it was a night that taught me the value of not taking the autonomy of my body for granted—a lesson learned in the most perplexing way possible.

After tossing and turning, I managed to find my way back to sleep, only to be nudged awake by a foreign and alarming sensation once again. My body, once a vessel of strength and coordination, betrayed me in those moments, leaving me struggling with a loss of control that was as frightening as it was sudden. The room spun, and my stomach stirred violently, leading to an inevitable encounter with the wastebasket my husband had placed beside our bed. "BOOM, I fell out of bed onto the floor."

Duawne's voice, full of concern and fear, broke through the haze of my discomfort. "What is going on? Be careful," he urged, but all I could muster was a shout of frustration and helplessness. Despite the chaos, I climbed back into bed, and sleep engulfed me once more, only to be woken by my caring husband's gentle offer of aspirin and breakfast. Time had slipped away; it was already the next day, November 20, 2021.

The ring of my phone cut through the silence—a friend checking in after our recent meeting at the lounge. Her question about Duawne's whereabouts seemed concerning as I struggled with the reality of my condition. The decision to go to the hospital came easily, yet I insisted on bathing first—a moment of normalcy before facing the unknown.

The Diagnosis

I called my mother, who resided out of state, and her voice was calm, a clear distinction from the storm raging within me. I informed her of our trip to the hospital. The drive to Beaumont Health, Farmington (now Corewell Health), was a blur, and we were met by the swift arrival of attendants with a wheelchair upon our arrival. The emergency room was a whirlwind of activity, and as I lay there awaiting the results of a CT scan, my faith was a lifeline among the fear.

The diagnosis was as immediate as it was shocking: a **STROKE**. How could this be? At my age, it seemed impossible, a verdict meant for someone else. Yet, an undeniable truth carried me to Beaumont Health, Royal Oak (now Corewell Health) for higher care. In the face of such disbelief, my trust in God remained unshaken, a strong foundation of hope as I navigated the treacherous waters of recovery.

This experience, though terrifying, served as a reminder of life's fragility and the unexpected turns it can take. It emphasizes the importance of listening to one's body and seeking help without hesitation as I reflect on that turbulent time, filled with gratitude for the support of my loved ones and the medical professionals who acted quickly to preserve my health. Through faith and resilience, I have learned to embrace each day with renewed appreciation, knowing that every moment is a gift not to be taken for granted.

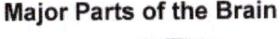

Major Parts of the Brain

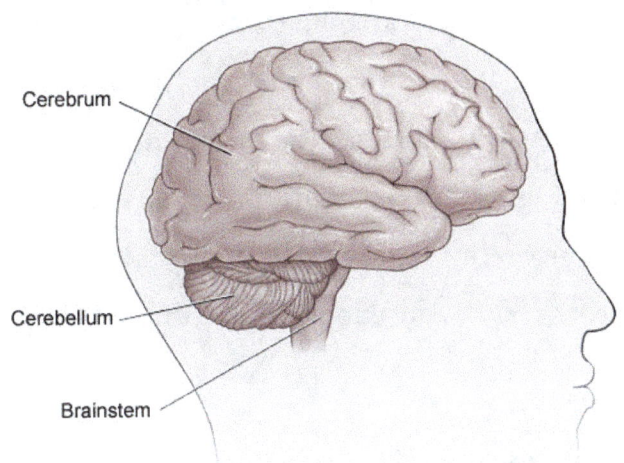

The sudden onset of a hemorrhagic stroke in the cerebellum is an event that can change one's life in an instant. The discovery of an arteriovenous malformation (AVM), a complex tangle of arteries and veins present from birth, can be shocking, especially when it has remained asymptomatic for years. The rupture leading to bleeding in the brain is a critical emergency that thrusts one into the whirlwind of urgent medical care.

Undergoing brain surgery to correct such a condition is an alarming anticipation. Yet, in my case, anticipating a six-hour procedure was completed in half the time, which I attribute to divine intervention. This profound experience reinforced my faith, feeling the presence of the Father, Son, and Holy Ghost throughout the tribulation.

The hospital stays, marked by significant challenges—loss of mobility, speech, writing ability, and impaired vision—became a period of deep spiritual reflection and growth. In the stillness of recovery, with the bustling world muted by the confines of a hospital room, the Lord's presence became more tangible, and my faith grew stronger.

This journey of healing was not just physical but also spiritual. Each small step in regaining second nature's functions was a testament to the resilience of the human body and spirit. The support of healthcare professionals, the prayers and encouragement from loved ones, and the personal conviction of faith all played crucial roles in my recovery.

Spending a month in the hospital, preparing for a craniotomy with AVM resection, was both overwhelming and frightening. The constant flow of doctors and medical information added to the anxiety, yet there was an underlying gratitude for being alive.

God showed grace to me by sparing my life. I knew I was about to embark on a new journey and decided that whatever came, I would choose life. I decided to do it because the Bible states, "I can do all things through Christ who strengthens me" (Philippians 4:13).

Encouragement: No matter how dark or overwhelming your circumstances may seem, remember that each day is an opportunity to choose life. Sometimes, life changes instantly, and what seemed stable becomes shaky, but within every challenge lies the power to transform. It's not easy to face uncertainty, to wake up with fear, or to question what comes next. But you have a **choice**—to let your challenges define you or to rise above them and let God's grace guide your steps.

CHOOSE to see the light in your situation, even if it's just a flicker. **CHOOSE** to trust God's timing, even when the path is unclear. No matter how difficult, your journey is filled with purpose and strength. Take each step with faith, knowing that you are not walking alone, even when you walk through the valleys. You are loved, held, and chosen for a reason more significant than any storm you will face.

Let my story remind you that you are stronger than you know. Let your story be proof that nothing can stand in the way of a person determined to live fully, faithfully, and without fear. Today is not just a new day; it's a chance to rewrite your story, breathe in the grace around you, and believe that better days are ahead. #BreatheSis

I challenge you today to make a declaration over your life by inserting your name and stating it aloud.

"I (YOUR NAME), hereby declare today I will **CHOOSE** to live intentionally, embrace opportunities, surround myself with positive influence, and believe in the promises of the Lord. I will speak of victory over every circumstance and expect a miracle. By **CHOOSING** life and not defeat, I am a living testimony of God's healing power, a walking miracle who inspires others to live purposefully and fearlessly. I understand life is a precious gift, and I **CHOOSE** to live. AMEN

https://es.pinterest.com/
pin/932104454127790172/

Stroke Stat: According to the CDC, someone in the U.S. has a stroke every 40 seconds. Stroke is a leading cause of death and disability. According to the American Stroke Association, approximately 795,000 people in the United States have a stroke each year, and about 1 in 4 of those are repeat strokes. (American Heart Association, 2023)

Reflection Questions:
1. How has God shown His grace in your life through difficult circumstances?
2. How did this experience change your perspective or your approach to challenges?
3. What does choosing life mean to you right now, and what is one action you can take today to affirm that choice?

Closing Prayer: Lord, I thank you for the gift of life and the strength to overcome challenges that once seemed difficult. You have walked with me through every step of my recovery, and I am forever grateful for your healing touch. Help me to continue choosing life every day, trusting that your grace is enough. May my story inspire others to see your goodness and find hope in you. Amen

CHAPTER 2

November 20, 2021: The Day Everything Changed

Self-Care Tip Box: *Find moments of stillness and breathe deeply. When the world feels overwhelming, take 5 minutes to focus on your breath, reflect, and recenter your thoughts. Remember, self-care is about honoring your mind, body, and spirit.*

Quote: You may encounter many defeats, but you must not be defeated. In fact, it may be necessary to encounter the defeats, so you can know who you are, what you can rise from, and how you can still come out of it." — Maya Angelou

Scripture Reading: I have told you all this so that you will have peace of heart and mind. Here on earth, you will have many trials and sorrows, but cheer up, for I have overcome the world" (John 16:33 TLB).

My Story: Life is unpredictable. You're perfectly fine one moment, and everything changes the next. A debilitating sickness was my reality on November 20, 2021. I was at home, looking forward to a relaxing evening, when suddenly, I was in an ambulance speeding toward Beaumont Health, Royal Oak (now Corewell Health).

My vision blurred, my speech slurred, and my right arm throbbed with pain. Walking was impossible, and understanding the diagnosis felt like deciphering a foreign language. Yet, despite the terrifying situation, my faith remained unshaken. I felt God's presence around me, guiding me through this storm.

I remember the paramedic turning to my husband, Duawne, and asking if he wanted to ride in the ambulance or follow behind. In a state of shock and disbelief, he chose to follow. It felt like we had been swept up in a tornado, and our lives had turned upside down instantly.

One moment, I was safe and comfortable in my own home, and the next, I was being carried away between hospitals for a neurosurgical evaluation. The suddenness was overwhelming, an absolute reminder of how quickly life can change.

This experience vividly demonstrated life's unpredictability and served as a testament to the power of faith and resilience. Despite the fear and uncertainty, I trusted in God's guidance and found strength in my belief.

I was reminded to hold on to my faith no matter what life threw my way. I trusted in the journey, even when the path was uncertain. I began to tell myself that I was strong, and with faith and resilience, I could weather this storm.

Following my diagnosis, I was admitted to the Intensive Care Unit. The presence of my mother, Nadine, and niece Miyia', who had flown in from Arizona at 4 a.m., provided much-needed comfort. Their reassuring words, the sight of flowers, and comforting prayers were a balm to my troubled spirit. It felt incredible to be surrounded by family. Their presence was a lifeline as I wrestled with the reality of my condition.

My physical state was challenging. Confined to bed, unable to bathe or urinate independently, I found myself reliant on medical assistance for the most basic tasks. A urinary catheter was inserted into my bladder to drain my urine, a procedure that left me feeling frustrated and in disbelief. "This can't be life," I thought to myself.

Adding to my discomfort was the embarrassment of being undressed by two nurses—one of whom was male—and positioned in the frog-leg stance for the catheter insertion. It was a difficult moment, one that tested my resilience and strength.

Yet, despite these challenges, I held onto my faith and the love of my family. Their unwavering support and the power of prayer gave me the strength to face each day, reminding me that even in our darkest moments, we are never alone.

Here are a few uplifting words that I would like to highlight: No matter what trials you may face, remember that you have the strength to overcome them. Hold on to your faith, lean on your loved ones, and trust the journey. It is through these trials that we discover our true character and identity.

A few days went by, and I was given a medical basin to expel my biles— "Talk about humiliation." Determined not to depend on medication, I requested a warm cup of water to help move the bile for quicker relief. In a predictable cycle, nurses came in and out of my room, administering medication and giving me an Enoxaparin injection in my abdomen to prevent blood clots. I became "accustomed" and "numb" to this new reality over the next 26 days. Despite feeling ashamed, I remained strong-willed through the routine changing of the catheter collection bag and sponge baths. Surrounded by a sense of paralysis, I reached for light, for my voice—a glimmer in the void—and prayed for the restoration of my vision. When will this end?

On November 21, 2021, an external ventricular drain (EVD) was inserted into my skull to relieve pressure on my brain. Being kept in a supine position with the head of the bed elevated for seven days was excruciating. Just before the procedure, I remember my cousin entering the ICU room as the doctor began drilling through the bone in my head, causing blood to splatter everywhere. Although I was awake, I didn't feel any pain. I recall the medical team loudly saying, "No, don't enter," and closing the curtain to prevent anyone from seeing. Over the following week, the EVD was clamped and removed, and I underwent a cerebral arteriogram for embolization of the AVM.

A Walking Miracle

The arrival of my mother at the hospital the following day brought a wave of relief. Her presence was like a soothing balm, providing the nurturing love and support I desperately needed during this challenging time. "Thank you, Lord," I whispered as she gently gave me a thorough sponge bath.

As I lay in the Intensive Care Unit, awaiting the results of my tests, a surgeon from the neurosurgery team entered to discuss the next steps in my treatment. The news he delivered was unexpected and alarming. I suffered a stroke due to a ruptured vermian arteriovenous malformation - a tangle of abnormal blood vessels connecting arteries and veins in the brain.

The surgeon seemed very surprised that I was coherent and communicating with him, given the severity of my condition. The ruptured vessel had led to a hemorrhage, causing a significant amount of blood to pool in my brain. Yet, here I was, conscious and engaging in conversation. He looked at me with a sense of wonder and remarked, "Wow, you are a MIRACLE!"

His words resonate deeply within me. Yes, **I AM A MIRACLE.** Despite the odds, I was fighting, surviving, and even thriving. This realization filled me with a renewed sense of hope and determination. I knew then that I would not let this medical crisis define me or dictate the course of my life.

This journey has taught me the power of faith, resilience, and vitality for life. It has shown me that miracles happen, often in the most unexpected ways. It has reinforced my belief in the power of love and support from my loved ones, which gave me the strength I needed to face even the most intimidating challenges.

My life-altering experience taught me many lessons. I want to offer a few points for you to consider. No matter what trials you may be facing, remember that you, too, are a miracle. Believe in your strength, hold onto your faith, and never underestimate the power of love and support. It is these elements that truly make miracles possible.

Suddenly, life can present situations that test our courage and faith. One such moment occurred when I was faced with a sudden medical emergency, leaving no time to question or hesitate over signing the pre-surgery release form.

As the surgeon began to detail the surgical procedure, I could see the nervousness creeping into my husband's eyes. The doctor discussed the team involved, the risks associated with the procedure, the expected recovery time, and the legal implications. He handed me a statement that essentially said I couldn't sue the medical office or the doctor if I were to be injured as a result of the surgery.

At that moment, I felt a wave of uncertainty wash over me. But then, I looked at my husband, and

I saw the trust he had in me. I realized that this was not a time for fear but a time for faith. With confidence swelling in my heart, I turned to the surgeon and said, "All I can do is trust GOD."

This statement may seem simple, but it carries a profound significance. It was a declaration of my faith, my belief in a higher power that guides us through the trials and tribulations of life. It was a testament to my resilience and determination to face whatever came my way with courage and optimism.

In times of crisis, we often find ourselves questioning everything. We wonder why we have been put in such situations and what our future holds. In these moments, we must remember to hold onto our faith, which gives us the strength to face our fears, overcome our challenges, and emerge stronger on the other side.

Remember to trust your faith, no matter what life throws at you. Believe in the power of positivity and the strength of your spirit. Most importantly, remember that you are never alone in your journey. There is always a higher power watching over you, guiding you, and giving you the strength to face whatever comes your way.

1 Peter 1:6-7 NLT So be truly glad. There is wonderful joy ahead, even though you must endure many trials for a little while. These trials will show that your faith is genuine. It is being tested as fire tests and purifies gold—though your faith is far more precious than mere gold. So when your faith remains strong through many trials, it will bring you much praise and, glory, and honor on the day when Jesus Christ is revealed to the whole world.

After giving my husband and me some time to pray and reflect on the impending procedure, the surgeon returned. He began recounting his conversation with the head neurosurgeon about our meeting. He told the head surgeon that he had reviewed the pre-surgery release form with us. The head surgeon responded in shock, "You mean her family?" He replied, "No, with the patient Menzaire Boykins-Esters."

The head neurosurgeon's response was one of astonishment. "Wow, she's a miracle. We haven't seen a patient coherent with blood on the brain in 30 years." His words mimicked what I had been feeling—I was a miracle, a testament to the power of faith and resilience.

I gave the surgeon consent by signing the papers with renewed confidence and without a shadow of a doubt. I trusted God, believed in the skill and expertise of the medical team, and held onto the love and support of my family.

This decision was not easy. It required enormous courage and faith. It also served as a reminder of my strength, the power of prayer, and the miracles that can happen when we trust the Lord.

Hold onto your faith no matter what challenges you may be facing. Trust in the journey, believe in prayer's power and never underestimate your strength and resilience. Through these trials, we discover our true potential and life's miracles.

Throughout every step of this journey, I felt God's presence with me. This morning, as I looked through my journal, reflecting on different scriptures and how far I had come, a sense of gratitude washed over me. I had truly overcome a giant who tried to take me out.

Recovery was not easy. My discharge papers estimated that I would need a walker for 13 months. However, I exceeded all expectations through continuous physical therapy, strength training, prayer, and absolute determination. On January 3, 2022, less than a month after discharge, I transitioned from a walker to a cane.

And just a short while later, I was walking on my own. This milestone was more than just a physical achievement; it was a testament to my determination.

This journey has taught me the true meaning of perseverance and the power of faith. It has shown me that no matter how insurmountable the odds may seem, we can overcome any obstacle with determination and trust in God.

Psalm 23:6 - Surely goodness and mercy shall follow me all the days of my life, and I shall dwell in the house of the Lord forever.

Encouragement: Letting your circumstances defeat you is easy, but there is power in choosing to rise above. You have the strength within you to overcome every storm. Focus on what you can control and let go of what you cannot. Life will have its setbacks, but when you learn to maintain an unshakeable spirit, telling yourself that all is well, you regain control of your happiness and peace. Let my testimony remind you how God can transform your life when you believe, trust, and wait on Him. Give yourself the grace to accept your new body. #BreatheSis

Stroke Stat: Strokes are the leading cause of severe long-term disability in adults. It's crucial to recognize the signs early and seek medical attention immediately. (American Stroke Association, 2023)

Source: American Stroke Association

Reflection Questions:

1. What strategies help you find peace and maintain hope when faced with an unexpected challenge?

2. What can you do today to nurture your body, mind, and soul as you navigate life's changes?

Closing Prayer: Good Morning, Holy Spirit; I'm so glad you're still with me, and most importantly, your love endures forever. I can't get enough of your love for me. Thank you for your new mercies every morning and for your goodness that continues to follow me throughout my life. I praise you because you said I'm forever loved, healed, strong, forgiven, adopted, whole, purposeful, hopeful, joyful, peace-filled, victorious, powerful, fearfully and wonderfully made, worthy, and yours. Thank you, Jesus, for walking me out of affliction and into the most remarkable season of my life! It begins today! In the name of Jesus, I declare these things to be so! Amen

CHAPTER 3

A Silent Threat: Understanding AVM

Self-Care Tip Box: *Educate yourself regarding your body and health. Understanding your condition can empower you, help you make informed decisions, and ease your journey toward recovery. Remember, knowledge is power, and self-awareness is self-care.*

Quote: "The greatest wealth is health, and the best way to protect it is through knowledge and continuous learning about your body." – Accredited to the Roman Poet, Virgil

Scripture Reading: Wisdom is the principal thing; Therefore, get wisdom. And in all your getting, get understanding (Proverbs 4:7 NKJV).

My Story: What is AVM? I was unfamiliar with it before, and I'm continually learning more about it. I want to share what I've discovered so far. An arteriovenous malformation (AVM) is a complex network of intertwined arteries and veins in the brain that interferes with normal blood circulation. It can develop in any part of the body, including the brain. Arteries transport oxygen-rich blood from the heart to the brain and other organs, while veins return oxygen-depleted blood to the lungs and heart. An AVM disrupts this essential process, potentially depriving nearby tissues of oxygen.

The abnormal formation of blood vessels in an AVM makes them prone to weakening and rupturing. If an AVM in the brain bursts, it can result in bleeding within the brain, leading to a stroke or brain damage. This type of bleeding is a hemorrhage.

Brain AVMs occur in less than 1% of the population. Surprisingly, it's more common in males than females. An increased prevalence has been seen in conditions such as Hereditary Hemorrhagic Telangiectasia (HHT). It is a genetic disorder in which blood vessels do not develop normally, leading to bleeding that can be serious or life-threatening. It's often hidden—a silent threat—until something catastrophic happens, like a stroke.

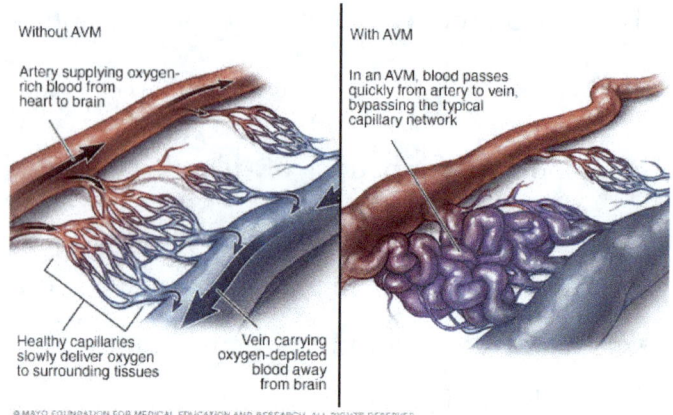

Without AVM

Artery supplying oxygen-rich blood from heart to brain

With AVM

In an AVM, blood passes quickly from artery to vein, bypassing the typical capillary network

Healthy capillaries slowly deliver oxygen to surrounding tissues

Vein carrying oxygen-depleted blood away from brain

© MAYO FOUNDATION FOR MEDICAL EDUCATION AND RESEARCH ALL RIGHTS RESERVED.

Arteriovenous malformation - Symptoms and causes - Mayo Clinic

On November 23, 2021, an arteriogram revealed that I had a right paramedian superior posterior fossa AVM measuring 1.8 x 1.2 x 0.5 cm, with blood supply from the left posterior inferior cerebellar artery (PICA).

Discovering that I had an AVM- especially one that had already ruptured and caused a stroke- was both shocking and overwhelming. Suddenly faced with trying to understand a condition I had never even heard of before. The exact cause of AVMs remains unclear, though in rare cases, they can be inherited within families.

My medical team, led by Dr. Staudt, performed a suboccipital craniectomy on December 3, 2021, to resect the complex AVM that had ruptured. During surgery, they worked carefully to access the AVM, protect critical blood vessels, and remove the tangled mass that had disrupted my life. The process was intense, with precision and care guiding every step.

I'm sharing these details because knowledge can help empower you, just as it did me. Understanding my condition gave me a sense of control over my journey. I hope you'll gain insight into my story and the silent conditions that can impact our health without warning.

AVMs often cause no symptoms until complications develop, such as brain hemorrhage or bleeding into the brain. Some AVMs may produce a swooshing sound that can be heard through a stethoscope. Other symptoms may include:

- Pulsing noise in the head
- Headache
- Progressive weakness or numbness

Some studies have suggested that patients may suffer from a seizure due to an AVM. These patients are at higher risk of hemorrhage. The studies also indicate that in the first year following a spontaneous AVM hemorrhage, the risk of bleeding again may be as high as 6% to 18%, which is four times higher than the initial risk.

If bleeding occurs, symptoms may include:

- Sudden, severe headache
- Weakness or numbness

- Vision loss
- Difficulty speaking
- Inability to understand others
- Severe unsteadiness

Acting quickly is essential if you experience sudden headaches, dizziness, and vomiting without a clear cause. It can be crucial if you don't recognize the F.A.S.T. signs of a stroke, such as facial drooping, arm weakness, speech difficulties, and the urgency to call emergency services. Head to the emergency room right away and request an MRI.

I didn't seek immediate medical attention, so let my experience serve as a warning. If I had gone sooner, I could have received treatment and potentially prevented the stroke. Most arteriovenous malformations (AVMs) are identified through a computed tomography (CT) brain scan or a magnetic resonance imaging (MRI) brain scan. For any AVM treatment, an angiogram may be necessary to understand the specific type of AVM better.

Despite my condition, it did not hold me back but motivated me to find purpose.

Encouragement: You may face something that feels bigger than you—something you don't understand. Know that you are not alone. While it may seem like a silent threat, bringing it to light to better understand it is your first step toward healing. The unknown can be frightening, but there is strength in learning about what you're facing.

Remember, challenges are not meant to break you but to build you. You can confront the unknown and navigate it with courage and faith. Educate yourself on your family history and get regular checkups. When you go to the doctor, ask questions and advocate for yourself. Most importantly, listen to your body, and don't ignore it. #BreatheSis

Stroke Stat: According to the National Institute of Neurological Disorders and Stroke, about 1 in 100,000 people experience an arteriovenous malformation (AVM). It is estimated that about 12% of AVMs lead to severe symptoms, such as brain hemorrhage, stroke, or seizures, often without any warning signs. Early detection is key to proper management and treatment.

(Source: National Institute of Neurological Disorders and Stroke, 2023)

Source: NINDS - AVM Information

Reflection Questions:

1. Reflect on when you felt overwhelmed by a diagnosis or life event. What happened? How did you handle it? Or are you in it now?

2. How can educating yourself bring peace or empowerment to your journey?

Closing Prayer: Father God, I come boldly to your throne, thanking you for loving me, thanking you for choosing me, and thanking you for saving me for such a time as this. Lord, your love has held me and kept me through the suffering. Your word says in Isaiah 43:2 ESV, "When you pass through the waters, I will be with you; and through the rivers, they shall not overwhelm you; when you walk through fire, you shall not be burned, and the flame shall not consume you." This promise assumes we will walk through fire—or difficult times. It isn't an *if,* it's a *when.* Laying in the operating room and holding on to your promise fulfilled me…trusting that I can face any obstacle with unwavering faith, knowing that you are with me. Your hope and healing led me quickly to a place of restoration. Oh Lord, your healing oil flows through me like a living stream. May my suffering be a testament to your healing power, and that my faith continues to grow deeper. In you, I put my trust. I understand the suffering was worth it because of what you are doing in my life, and I will continue to praise you. Amen

CHAPTER 4

The Power of
Prayer and People

Self-Care Tip Box: Your inner circle plays a significant role in your physical, mental, and emotional recovery. It provides a stable and uplifting environment that helps you rebuild your resilience, maintain a positive mindset, and navigate challenging times.

Quote: "The powerful promise of God's presence when we pray with others is too great a gift to ignore." — Stormie Omartian

Scripture Reading: "I also tell you this: If two of you agree here on earth concerning anything you ask, my Father in heaven will do it for you" (Matthew 18:19, NLT).

My Story: People are important, and I was fortunate to have some incredible individuals around me. My inner circle was crucial to my recovery, standing by me during the most challenging period of my life with encouragement and support. They became the strong foundation I needed when I could no longer be the strong one myself. With their help, I developed a more positive outlook on my recovery. They tirelessly drove me to every doctor's appointment and physical, occupational, and speech therapy session for a year without a single complaint.

Having my fantastic husband and lovely mother as part of my inner circle has been an incredible blessing. I can't imagine where I would be without their gentle and loving support. We've shared countless evenings filled with prayer, praise, scrabble games, card games, memory match challenges, puzzles, and physical activities that have kept me motivated and determined to persevere.

A cherished memory I will always hold dear is when my mother and I performed dance routines together to challenge my mind and restore balance. Dancing became a regular part of my daily routine, helping to lift my spirits whenever I felt down or defeated. Research indicates that dancing releases endorphins, neurotransmitters that enhance happiness and well-being, improving mood and a sense of euphoria. The Joy of Dancing: Mental Health Benefits

The Lord guided me to the "Help A Sister Stand" women's group during a particularly challenging time in my life, and the sense of connection with this community of women was incredible. My mother, Nadine, and friend, Kristal, who are members, invited me to join their powerful prayer line, where I had the chance to share my testimony about the Lord's goodness in saving my life. That evening gave me fulfillment and helped me recognize my divine purpose. I knew the Lord was intricately involved.

"Help A Sister Stand" is a faith-based women's group where I discovered genuine sisterhood. We connect weekly on the prayer line and meet monthly in person, finding upliftment, encouragement, and strength through the word of God.

One key point I'd like to emphasize is the immense power and benefit of friendships among women.

Since joining "Help A Sister Stand," I've learned much from other women, including praying for my husband's spiritual growth, emotional well-being, and professional success as a wife. Our motto is teaching women how to love themselves.

Help A Sister Stand

I Am Somebody

I Am Woman

I Am Fearfully and Wonderfully Made

I Am Beautiful on The Inside and the Outside

I hold this motto near and dear to my heart. However, as women, we often hesitate to fully embrace the essence of true sisterhood. This reluctance is frequently influenced by societal teachings on how we should treat or perceive one another, misconceptions we've accepted about our gender's ability to get along, low self-esteem, insecurity, and personal ego. As women, we need to rise and affirm the sisterhood we are meant to experience because the reality is that **WE NEED EACH OTHER**.

We are undoubtedly more powerful when united! If we notice our sister facing challenges in any aspect of her life, we should feel empowered to approach her, offer our prayers, listen attentively, and encourage her.

"Rich is the person who has a praying friend."
~Janice Hughes

During my recovery, I sought a safe and supportive environment for community and healing, where I could build resilience and confidence. I joined the S.H.E (She Has Everything) healing circle for empowerment and Good Vibz yoga for meditation and physical health improvement. In the healing circles, I noticed my fear dissipated, and I gained more confidence in speaking publicly as I shared my testimony. I was no longer afraid to share my experiences, even if I struggled with pronunciation. I felt no shame, knowing that my story could help others.

Alongside the women's group and healing circle, I was fortunate to have a solid foundation of genuine friends who enriched my life with lunch and dinner outings, trips to baseball and football games, and even helped me plant a garden. Some incredible friends gave me movie tickets, invited me to yoga classes, treated me to massages, and introduced me to canoeing. Feeling appreciated and valued by such wonderful friends was genuinely uplifting.

Proverbs 17:17 (NASB) *A friend loves at all times, and a brother is born for adversity.*

As I healed, much was revealed. So-called friends who I thought should have been by my side began to show me their true selves. I realized they never were true friends from the beginning because they weren't there when I needed them the most. They showed no interest in our friendship, inconsistent communication, and conditional support. Some stopped receiving my calls, and it was emotionally tumultuous for me. I thought they were my true friends who provided the love, support, and encouragement I needed. I found out the feelings were not mutual. Reminded that many ships sail in the sea of life. Friendships, companionships, hardships, and relationships, as reality set in, I realized their season for friendships was over.

"A friend who stands with you in pressure is more valuable than a hundred ones who stand with you in pleasure."
— Edward G. Bulwer Lytton.

I began to see family from a different perspective. Very few extended a helping hand. The only emotion I could feel was disbelief. Wasn't I the person who extended the raft out to everyone during turbulence in their ocean? I found myself speaking my hurt feelings from my heart, hoping that people would understand my point of view. Unfortunately, that was not the case. Family and friends became offended and disassociated themselves from me, making it hard for me to attend gatherings. I began to set boundaries, which led to isolation. My boundaries became strong walls that isolated me and brought me into myself. It was conscious knowledge. The process was painful, but it led me to greater self-awareness.

1 John 2:19 NIV says, "They went out from us, but they did not really belong to us. For if they had belonged to us, they would have remained with us, but their going showed that none of them belonged to us."

The seven stages of grief include shock, denial, and anger. I found myself stuck in anger, resenting the circumstances that led to the loss of a life I once knew. It is rarely mentioned how anger can persist even after experiencing all stages of grief. Despite this, I hold on to my faith more firmly than my anger. The protective guard I mentioned helped me regain conscious awareness and can also become a barrier preventing blessings and new connections. I pray for the Lord's healing and knowing when to lower my defenses. I ask for the grace of God to forgive to surround me, making it unbearable to cling to the pain and emotions I'd grown used to.

This season has shown me the importance of being purposeful in every aspect of my life, whether accepting invitations, spending time with family and friends, or reaching out to others. I now rely on the guidance of the Holy Spirit in all areas of my life. When He says "GO," I go; when He advises against it, I refrain. Living with intention has become incredibly significant to me.

- According to the Bible, "living intentionally" means actively pursuing a life that aligns with God's will by making conscious choices in every aspect of life to honor and glorify God. Essentially, living a life with purpose and direction as guided by scripture means deliberately choosing actions that reflect your faith and values rather than passively going through life.

Tips on intentional living:
- **Follow God's Plan (Read your WORD).**
- **Actively engage your faith through daily choices.**
- **Make sure your actions and the people you choose to be around glorify God.**

Ephesians 5:10 is a great example. It is often cited as a key verse regarding intentional living, stating, "Find out what pleases the Lord."

I made it a habit to declare and memorize God's promises every morning. Scan here to download it for free. I share it here, hoping you will adopt it as a new habit.

Encouragement: No matter what happens throughout this season in your life, God has your back. There is beauty in being misunderstood, insulted, rejected, unsupported and unseen by people. It teaches you to rely on God for everything. #BreatheSis

Psalm 118:8-14 "It is better to trust in the LORD than to put confidence in man."

Stroke Stat: Research indicates that social support significantly enhances recovery outcomes for stroke survivors. A study published in the *Journal of Rehabilitation Research and Development* found that individuals with strong social networks experience better physical and psychological recovery post-stroke. These individuals are more likely to engage in rehabilitation, adhere to treatment plans, and report higher quality of life. (https://www.mayoclinic.org/diseases-conditions/stroke/in-depth/stroke-rehabilitation/art-20045172)

Reflection Questions:

1. Do you worry about your life and the future? Why or why not?

2. What support systems did you rely on to help you navigate through it?

Closing Prayer: Thank you, Lord, for granting me wisdom and meaningful connections and refining my relationships. May ego, fear of loss, and pride not obstruct my path to fulfilling my calling. I pray that the Holy Spirit's power breaks every chain of anger, revenge, and blame that holds me back. I welcome new connections that align with Your perfect will. In Jesus' name, Amen.

CHAPTER 5

Craniotomy and the Road to Recovery

> **Self-Care Tip Box:** *Whatever challenge you are facing this season, know it is divinely appointed, and nothing is wasted.*

Quote: "You're going to bounce back stronger than ever!" - Menzaire Boykins-Esters

Scripture Reading: For I will [a] restore you to [b] health And I will heal you of your wounds,' declares the Lord (Jeremiah 30:17, NASB).

My Story: On December 3rd, I underwent a left suboccipital craniectomy to excise the AVM. The procedure required shaving a portion of the scalp for an incision, removing a section of bone from the skull, sealing off, and extracting the AVM.

Afterward, the bone flap was reattached, and my incision was closed with 20 staples. The procedure was a significant and complex surgery.

I wasn't particularly nervous on the morning of my surgery. I felt confident in the days and weeks leading up to it, although my husband seemed more anxious than I was. My faith strengthened through numerous experiences with the Lord, and I trusted Him in every aspect of my life. His word promises to be a comforter in need, and I held onto that assurance. However, I can't fully explain how or why I was convinced that God would guide me through it. This surgery was no exception. I had witnessed His miraculous healing power before and was confident He would support me supernaturally. My life was in His hands.

I recall my mother quoting Matthew 9:20-22 over my bedside:

A woman who had been bleeding for 12 years came up behind Jesus in a crowd and touched the edge of his cloak. She believed that if she touched his clothes, she would be healed. Jesus turned around and said, "Daughter, be encouraged!" Affirming her faith and her healing.

I hid that scripture in my heart while in the hospital as a source of comfort and faith for me during this difficult time. So, when the day of the surgery came, the Holy Spirit gave me peace, laying in the preoperative holding area, quoting every scripture that came to remembrance. *Your word says you will never leave me nor forsake me.* I knew He would show up because that was my experience with Him. I also found additional comfort in the healing experience of others, like my aunt from breast cancer.

Because of my unwavering faith, the scriptures I kept on the inside, the undying support from my family and friends near and far, and the seat I've always had in the palm of God's hands, I was now prepped and pushed through the doors of my healing journey; the operating room.

The surgical theater transformed into a meticulous workshop. Mrs. Boykins Esters, tucked away by sterile drapes, became the canvas for a delicate masterpiece. Anesthesia, a gentle whisper, lulled her into slumber

as tubes, like silver threads, wove a lifeline. The Mayfield pins, like tiny anchors, secured her head as the surgeon charted a course through the landscape of her scalp.

The incision, a precise whisper of the scalpel, parted the skin like a curtain, revealing the bony stage beneath. The surgeon, a sculptor with steel instruments, carefully chipped away at the occipital bone, revealing the delicate brain within. Like gentle hands, retractors held back the cerebellar curtains, exposing the tangled threads of the AVM, a crimson spiderweb clinging to the brain's surface.

The microscope, a powerful lens, magnified the scene, transforming the surgical field into a vast, intricate world. The surgeon, guided by the roadmap of pre-operative imaging, navigated the treacherous terrain, meticulously dissecting the AVM's tendrils. Tiny clips, like miniature clothespins, stemmed the flow of blood as the surgeon, with the precision of a jeweler, *cauterized and divided the feeding arteries. The indocyanine green, a vibrant emerald dye, illuminated the blood flow, highlighting the remaining errant vessels like rogue stars in a darkened sky.*

The clot, a dark bruise on the brain's surface, was gently evacuated, revealing the healthy tissue beneath. The draining vein, a vital river, was carefully protected as the surgeon continued the painstaking dissection. Finally, freed from its moorings, the AVM was excised and sent to the laboratory, a captured villain under microscopic scrutiny.

The surgeon, having meticulously dismantled the crimson web, began the reconstruction process. The dural onlay, a silken patch, and the sealant, a protective glaze, sealed the delicate brain. Layer by layer, the surgeon closed the incision, stitching together the landscape of skin and muscle. Like tiny silver stitches, the staples sealed the wound, marking the end of the intricate performance.

Mrs. Boykins Esters, her journey through the surgical landscape complete, was gently awakened and returned to the world, the crimson spider web vanquished, a testament to the surgeon's artistry and skill.

Reading about the procedure gave me chills; realizing that my body had endured such a challenging and life-threatening experience was astonishing. I am genuinely thankful for the guidance provided by the surgeons and doctors, as well as for the advancements in medicine and technology. This experience has given me a deeper appreciation for life. Every day is a blessing, and every moment is an opportunity to embrace life with gratitude. I am incredibly grateful for all the prayers offered on my behalf.

Following the intense surgery, my family surrounded me with love and comfort. A nurse training to become a surgeon provided solace through her worship and praise of the Lord. The Bible mentions that we may entertain angels without knowing it, and during those challenging days after my surgery, she was the angel I needed.

Although I endured a challenging season, I want to encourage you, as I mentioned earlier, that God is our refuge in times of trouble. The challenges I faced are now being used in my life in ways I never imagined. Trust that God can use what you're going through for your good and His glory- allow Him to work through it.

Illness occurs, and surgeries are a daily reality; our lives are not under our control. Over the past two years, I've undergone intensive speech, physical, and occupational therapy sessions that have pushed me to my limits. I could have succumbed to fear or dwelled on all the negative possibilities, but instead, I chose to place my trust in God.

I've surrendered myself to Him, including all my worries. Self-care is essential, and this year, I'm focusing on myself. I've been through the fire and emerged as refined gold.

Encouragement: Never get tired of praying because God is always listening. I encourage you to trust God. I don't care what you are dealing with. He can do it. It is all for a divine purpose. #BreatheSis

Stroke Stat: There are over 7 million stroke survivors who live in United States and two-thirds of them are currently disabled. Around 25% of people who recover from their first stroke will have another within 5 years.

80% OF STROKES ARE PREVENTABLE!

Source: Stroke Facts & Statistics

Reflection Questions:

1. Reflecting on your own life, what challenges have you faced that have tested your faith, and how did you lean on God for strength during those times of weakness?

2. In your journey, what has been your most significant source of comfort when facing major challenges or health crises, and how can you apply that trust in God to other areas of your life?

3. After reading about my experience with surgery and recovery, how do you view the connection between faith and healing, and what new perspective do you have in your own struggles or times of uncertainty?

Closing Prayer: Lord, we pray for healing and restoration. Touch [Name] with Your healing hand and grant them renewed strength each day.

May their body respond positively to treatments and therapies, and may their mind find peace and clarity.

In Your holy name, we pray, Amen.

CHAPTER 6

Life After the Stroke

Self-Care Tip Box: *Healing is not a race but a process. Self-healing is not a journey but a destination. Literally, give yourself time to heal.*

Quote: "A setback is a setup for a comeback"- T.D. Jakes

Scripture Reading: "But blessed is the one who trusts in the Lord, whose confidence is in him.

They will be like a tree planted by the water that sends out its roots by the stream. It does not fear when heat comes; its leaves are always green. It has no worries in a year of drought and never fails to bear fruit" (Jeremiah 17:7-8, NIV)

My Story: When I think about life after my stroke, the words of Jeremiah 17:7-8 echo in my spirit. I first held onto that scripture while lying in the hospital bed, unsure of what the future would hold. Today, I live with the full assurance of hope in God. Yes, life has changed, but that isn't necessarily bad. I've found myself living a "new normal" that consists of a deeper reliance on God and a stronger relationship with Him.

Each morning, I wake up and sit with Him. I pray and wait for a word. Often, He speaks, guiding me through my day. I journal what He shares with me, taking time to process my thoughts and feelings—a practice I didn't have before the stroke.

Now, my days are marked by intentionality, both spiritually and physically. Living intentionally, for me, is setting a goal each day that I diligently set out to accomplish by the end of the week, leading to a fulfilled life. Each month, I set out to achieve a new activity that I've never done or an activity I've struggled with since my stroke.

Physically, the stroke took a toll on my body. I had to relearn how to speak and use my motor skills. My body now works at 90% capacity, but I am grateful for every progress. Praise God, I was discharged from the hospital with no medication. I still deal with stiffness in my neck and arm, so I prioritize massages to manage it. When I get angry, my right side stiffens—a reminder to calm down and prioritize peace. I also stretch in the mornings and make time for the gym. Every movement is a victory, and I celebrate the progress, no matter how small it may seem.

Mentally, I am more aware of the importance of authentic connections with people. I no longer take relationships lightly, as I've learned how precious life is. Emotionally, I find myself more in touch with my feelings. Often, I think about how fragile life is and the people who matter most to me.

One of the greatest lessons I've learned is to embrace gratitude. Every day, I give thanks for the significant victories and the small, everyday moments that once went unnoticed. Whether it's walking a little farther than I could last month or spending time with loved ones, I see the beauty in it all.

Socially, I've connected meaningfully with other survivors in the community. I work with the American Heart Association, participate in community events, and seek opportunities to give back. Sharing my testimony with others has been a source of healing for me. It reminds me that I'm not alone and that there's purpose in the pain I've endured.

The stroke awakened something in me spiritually. It deepened my faith and my understanding of God's grace. I rely on Him more than I ever did, knowing that His strength is made perfect in my weakness.

A stroke changes you in ways you might not expect. It shifts how you see the world, yourself, and your purpose. While the journey hasn't been easy, I know I am stronger, more intentional, and more grateful because of it.

Encouragement

A stroke isn't the end of the story. In fact, it can be the beginning of a new chapter filled with resilience, purpose, and joy. The journey may be challenging, but it is also an opportunity to rebuild your life based on faith, hope, and intentionality.

Healing is not linear. There will be good and hard days, but every day is a chance to lean into God's strength and grace. Your life matters. Your story matters. And there is so much more ahead of you than what lies behind you. #BreatheSis

Stroke Stat: According to the American Heart Association, stroke is a leading cause of death and disability among women in the United States. In 2021, stroke caused 162,890 deaths, with women accounting for approximately 57% of these fatalities. This statistic underscores the significant impact of stroke on women's health, highlighting the critical need for awareness, prevention, and support for those affected (American Heart Association, 2024).

Reflection Questions:

1. How has your understanding of the physical, emotional, and mental challenges faced by stroke survivors evolved after learning about the different ways a stroke can affect a person's life?

2. In what ways do you think stroke awareness, especially within specific communities, can be improved to support early prevention and better outcomes for survivors?

3. Reflect on a time in your life when you or someone close to you experienced a significant health challenge. How did you navigate the emotional and mental changes that came with it, and what lessons can be applied to supporting stroke survivors in their journey?

Closing Prayer:

Heavenly Father,

We come before You with hearts full of gratitude for the gift of life and the resilience You place within us. Lord, we thank You for Your strength that carries us through moments of weakness and for Your peace that surpasses all understanding.

For every stroke survivor reading this, I ask for Your healing touch to rest upon their bodies, minds, and spirits. Surround them with Your comfort and give them the courage to face each day with hope and determination. Let them feel Your presence in their recovery and remind them that they are never alone.

Lord, I pray that You continue to guide us to see purpose in our pain, to find joy in our journey, and to use our testimonies to bring encouragement to others. Teach us to live each day with intention, to love deeply, and to walk in the confidence that comes from trusting in You.

We declare that setbacks will not define us, but through Your power, they will set us up for a more significant comeback. We praise You for being the author of our stories and for the good plans You have for our future.

In Jesus' name, Amen.

 **CHAPTER 7**

Living with Purpose

Self-Care Tip Box: *Living with purpose means aligning your actions with God's plan for your life. Take time to listen for His guidance, and trust that every step you take, no matter how small, is a part of your divine journey. Be intentional with your time and always seek opportunities to serve others.*

Quote: "Your purpose is not just something you do; it's something you become. Walk in your calling with confidence-" Dr. Myles Munroe.

Scripture Reading: Then I heard the voice of the Lord saying, "Whom shall I send? And who will go for us?" And I said, 'Here am I. Send me!" (Isaiah 6:8, NIV)

My Story: I still vividly remember the first time I stepped into a leadership role. In March 2022, I led my first women's Zoom webinar in honor of International Women's Month. The topic was "What is Sisterhood?" This was a defining moment for me, as I shared my heart and encouraged women to embrace the power of supporting one another.

The following year, I held my first Stroke Awareness event in May, followed by a second one in May 2024. These events became more than just gatherings; they were platforms for me to raise awareness about strokes and their impact on women, particularly in the African American community.

These experiences have been both empowering and humbling. They have allowed me to use my voice to advocate for issues close to my heart, to educate others about the realities of stroke, and to inspire women to support each other in their journeys.

My voice matters. What I learned during the webinar from other women can be used to advocate my beliefs, educate women, and inspire change. Through these actions, we can make a difference in our communities and the lives of those around us.

On January 1, 2024, I led my first vision board party with my family. We displayed our goals, dreams, and aspirations for the new year, creating a tangible representation of our hopes for the future.

Later that month, on January 27, I was honored to facilitate another vision board party. This time, I introduced the Wheel of Life at an event hosted by Help A Sister Stand, themed 'Love Yourself Girl.' The ladies wrote their vision for the year, defining their goals and manifesting their dreams and desires. It was a fulfilling experience, being able to inspire and motivate these women by sharing my story and demonstrating how I've used the Wheel of Life over the years.

In June 2023, I walked in my purpose at my first American Heart Association Stroke and Heart Walk. This was an emotional experience, seeing so many people united for the exact cause. It ignited determination and a sense of advocacy inside of me. I walk because I know that with every step, I am saving lives. I am not only a stroke survivor, but I'm an advocate for stroke patients, survivors, and caregivers.

In June 2024, I returned to lead my team, uniting friends, family, and supporters for a cause close to my heart. Raising funds helps for lifesaving science. Science that can create an artificial heart valve. Prevent a life-threatening stroke. Put scientific advances into doctors' hands—correct heart defects in precious newborn babies. And someday, prayerfully, find a cure for high blood pressure. Science that can teach us all how to live longer and healthier lives.

These experiences have shown me the power of community, the importance of setting clear goals, and the impact we can make when we walk in our purpose. So, no matter what trials you may be facing, remember to set your sights on your goals, lean on your community, and never underestimate the power of living with purpose, for it is through these actions that we can make a difference in our lives and the lives of those around us.

Intrigued by the number of individuals not trained in our community or unaware of how to perform CPR. I am now a trained and certified First Aid/ CPR/AED Instructor. As a trained survivor, I'm excited to be educated and equipped to train our community. My mission is to empower, educate, and inspire other stroke survivors to let them know that there is life after a stroke.

In September 2024, I had the opportunity to share my pre-recorded story as an American Heart Association featured survivor at the Detroit Cycle Nation. This event showcased true inspiration, incredible strength, and resilience, helping to create real change in the fight against stroke and heart disease.

The following month, in October 2024, I was invited to attend the American Heart Association

Heart Ball as a survivor. It was such an honor to be in a room filled with so many influential people who were working towards the same goal: raising awareness and funds to fight heart disease and stroke. This experience reinforced my commitment to this cause and reminded me of the power of collective action.

Attending the "Love Yourself For Life Heart and Stroke Camp" is one of the most fulfilling moments of my journey so far. In August 2023, I attended my first camp in Port Huron, MI, followed by a second camp in Grass Lake, MI, in August 2024. These camps have been transformative, not only for me but for everyone involved. They've given me the tools to help others who are walking the same path I've walked.

In January 2024, I was also honored to be aired on FOX 2 News as a stroke survivor celebrating National Heart Health Month. While promoting the Love Yourself 4 Life 9th Annual Heart & Stroke "Go Red" Fundraiser held in February, I was crowned LY4L 2024 survivor Queen and given year-long perks from the Love Yourself 4 Life non-profit organization—free tickets to events, etc.

The journey continued, and I was invited to attend the Detroit Heart Walk Executive Breakfast in January 2024, where I learned how to continue to get involved in the fight for heart and stroke awareness. It has been a life-changing experience to be a part of such powerful initiatives.

December 3, 2024: Nominated for the American Heart Association Stroke Hero Award. It was indeed an honor to receive an email from one of the AHA directors informing me that I was nominated. Every year, the American Heart Association does its annual Stroke Hero Awards that honor individuals in the community who have shown resilience and outstanding progress.

I also attend the Henry Ford Stroke Support Group every 2nd Wednesday. This group has become an integral part of my life, providing me with a platform to stay connected with my community and increase my participation in social activities.

The group serves as another pillar of support, a safe space where we can all share our recovery journeys. We learn from each other's experiences, draw strength from our collective resilience, and find comfort in knowing we are not alone in our struggles.

Being part of this group has reinforced my belief in the power of community and the healing potential of shared experiences. It has shown me that while our journeys may be unique, the challenges we face and the triumphs we celebrate bind us together.

Lastly, my most recent adventure was my first mission trip to Kenya, Africa, in October 2024.

That trip reminded me how far I've come and how much more there is to do. I returned feeling like I had a deeper understanding of my calling to serve and uplift others.

As 2024 came to a close, I found myself walking in purpose, with purpose. I was given the opportunity to join the Knuckles Health Education Services to Life team to initiate a heart and stroke survivorship support group. Starting January 2025, we meet every Wednesday. As the support coordinator, I aim to help survivors with disabilities or special needs access services and support to improve their quality of life.

Our mission is to strengthen the lives of heart and stroke survivors, friends, family, and caregivers through education, support, fellowship, and encouragement. Working closely with individuals and their families, we strive to help them rebuild their lives after a stroke or heart injury.

This role has given me a renewed sense of purpose. It's more than just a job; it's a calling. It allows me to use my experiences to help others navigate their journeys, providing them with the support and resources they need to overcome their challenges.

Living with purpose provides a compass for our actions, fuels our passions, and, ultimately, a deeper meaning to our existence. It reminds us that we are part of something bigger and that our struggles and triumphs can be a light of hope for others.

So, remember to hold onto your faith no matter what trials you face. Trust in your journey, believe in your strength, and never underestimate the power of living with purpose. It is through these trials that we discover our true potential and the miracles that life has in store for us.

Walk in purpose,
WITH PURPOSE.

ENCOURAGEMENT: CHOOSE life daily by living purposefully, aligning your choices and actions with your passions and core values. Most importantly, creating a life that is meaningful and of substance. There is only one thing you should not waste: **LIFE.**

"Celebrate your progress, no matter how big or small, as you move towards a life of purpose." #BreatheSis

Stroke Stat: According to the Centers for Disease Control and Prevention (CDC), nearly 800,000 people in the United States have a stroke each year. Of those, about 140,000 die, making stroke the fifth leading cause of death in the U.S. Stroke is also a leading cause of long-term disability, with many survivors facing challenges in physical, emotional, and social recovery (CDC, 2022).

Reflection Questions:

1. What are some ways you can align your current actions with the purpose God has called you to, and how can you begin to walk in that purpose with confidence?

2. How can you use your personal experiences, no matter how difficult, to inspire and

support others who may be going through similar struggles?

3. Think about the key moments in your life when you felt God calling you to serve or make a difference. How can you take those experiences and create meaningful change in your community or beyond?

Closing Prayer: Dear Heavenly Father,

We come before You today with open hearts and minds, seeking Your guidance as we strive to live our lives purposefully. We ask that You illuminate our paths and guide our steps, leading us towards the plans You have for us.

Help us to recognize the unique gifts and talents You have bestowed upon us, and show us how to use them to serve others and glorify Your name. May we always remember that our purpose is not just about personal fulfillment but also about making a difference in the lives of those around us.

Grant us the courage to step out in faith, even when the path ahead seems uncertain. Help us to trust in Your timing, knowing that You have a plan for every season of our lives.

When we face challenges and obstacles, remind us of Your promise in Jeremiah 29:11 that You have plans to prosper us and not to harm us, plans to give us hope and a future. Let this promise fuel our determination and resilience as we continue to walk in our purpose.

Above all, may we seek to do Your will in all things, living our lives in a way that reflects Your love and grace. Help us to be a light in this world, showing others the way to You through our actions and words.

In Jesus' name, we pray. Amen.

CHAPTER 8

Lessons from the Valley

Self-Care Tip Box: When you're at a low point, listen to God rather than seeking advice from others. This is crucial because it offers clarity, reassurance, and comfort when you feel lost.

Quote: "It's the journey through the valleys that shapes us into who we are." Menzaire Boykins-Esters

Scripture Reading: "Trust in the Lord with all your heart and lean not on your own understanding; in all your ways submit to him, and he will make your paths straight" (Proverbs 3:5-6 NIV).

My Story: Sometimes, we travel on a journey we never imagined. And that journey is life. In this life, we will experience twists and turns and may even end up in the valley—where I found myself alone and in disbelief. An unknown place where a reservation was never made, bags were never packed, hair and nails were never done but still headed in the valley. The valley is a place where I met fire and pressure and came out as pure **GOLD.**

The most disconcerting thing about walking through dark valleys is the uncertainty. When you're walking in the shadows, you have no way of knowing the unseen. It's frightening. The reassuring part was that I was not traveling alone.

God was always with me. David, who also found himself in a valley, wrote: *"Yea, though I walk through the valley of the shadow of death, I will fear no evil: FOR THOU ART WITH ME; thy rod and thy staff they comfort me"* (Psalm 23:4, KJV).

While in the valley, I gained an appreciation for life and insight into my purpose and took a brave stand in my relationship with God. As James wrote: *"My brethren, COUNT IT ALL JOY when ye fall into divers' temptations; Knowing this, that the trying of your faith worketh patience. But let patience have her perfect work, that ye may be perfect and entire, wanting nothing"* (James 1:2-4, KJV).

There was joy in the valley because the Lord worked in my life daily during my healing. I was amazed at how fast God was answering my prayers.

At 39, I found myself helpless, having to learn how to walk, talk, drive, write, type, and sing again.

Every valley is different, and there are new lessons to learn from each of them in our lives.

Here are some of the lessons that the Lord taught me as I traveled through this valley:

1. During my journey through the valley, I understood the true essence of walking by faith. It was not until my faith was tested that I truly understood the meaning of walking by faith, not by sight. We don't learn to walk by faith by attending church, listening to sermons, or reading daily devotionals. The school of theology is taught in the depths of the darkest valley, not on the mountaintop. While in the valley, God revealed a comforting message of truth and the true meaning of Jehovah Jireh, my provider. On December 26, 2021, I applied for Social Security disability benefits, believing I was

eligible and could never work again because of my health challenge. I prayed and told the Lord this was only temporary, and I would be back in the workplace.

Uncertain how I was going to pay my bills, I filed for short-term disability in January of 2022. Thank God I had Aflac supplemental insurance to help cover expenses while my husband paid all the other household expenses.

Within a month, I began receiving income from short-term disability. I felt a sense of relief knowing that I was able to contribute to our household, focus on recovery, and reduce my husband's stress level. In disbelief, I received a response letter from Social Security in August of the same year stating that I didn't qualify for benefits on the claim and was denied, which turned out to be a blessing in disguise. One thing to remember is that God's lesson plans for us may involve many trials, like

Job, when he lost his wealth, family, and health. Whether it's fiery furnaces or a journey through the valley, it's crucial to maintain a strong foundation in God.

The Bible states in Psalm 66:19: "But God has surely listened and has heard my prayer."

2. I also discovered the importance of relationships during my time in the valley. I am grateful to understand that relationships hold more value than to-do lists, projects, and personal plans. I am intentional about calling loved ones on the phone and scheduling lunch dates. This valley experience has really taught me how to evaluate genuine relationships and how to rely on others during challenging times by letting go of my pride. True friends were revealed, offering love and support and consistently showing up daily. When you experience any potentially life-threatening

or life-changing illness, your perspective on what's important shifts.

"Count no day unimportant if you still have each other, for the day will come when you would give everything for just one day, any ordinary day you once shared together."

—unknown author.

3. Lastly, I learned God is there, too, in the valley.

Laying silently in the bed, I began to recite.

Psalm 23:4 *Even though I walk through the valley of the shadow of death, I will fear no evil, for you are with me. Thank you, Lord, for you are with me. You are with me.* I repeatedly told myself. Affirming that he was with me gave me incredible assurance. What else did I need to know? His words confirmed that he was with me while in the valley. That's all I need.

A peace engulfed me, and I repeated it again, this time in a triumphant declaration of faith: *You are with me! You are with me! You are with me! Praise the Lord.*

Encouragement: Some have said, "If you're not headed out of a valley, you're headed into one." When you don't know which way to turn or how you will make it out, look to the hills that come with your help. Your help cometh from the Lord Psalm 121. Remember, optimism does not deny reality; it's an attitude one deals with. Let's trust God to see us through from the valley's entrance—even if we're just crawling—until we're dancing out the exit, praising the Lord for what he has done. #BreatheSis

Stroke Stat: Hemorrhagic strokes make up about 13% of stroke cases. They occur when a weakened vessel ruptures and bleeds into the surrounding brain. The blood accumulates and compresses the surrounding brain tissue.

The two types of hemorrhagic strokes are intracerebral hemorrhage (within the brain) and subarachnoid hemorrhage (between the inner and outer layers of the tissue covering the brain). (American Heart Association, 2025) Hemorrhagic Stroke | American Stroke Association

Reflection Questions:

1. As you wake to another morning, do you feel relieved from trouble or weighed down by it?
2. You may be experiencing some mountaintop moments, and mornings are a delight, but mornings can be difficult when you are in a valley.

Whatever your experience is right now, remember that God has redeemed you. Psalm 111:9 NIV: "He provided redemption for his people; he ordained his covenant forever- holy and awesome is his name."

Closing Prayer: Heavenly Father, In this darkest hour, I cling to your presence, knowing that you are my shepherd leading the way and I lack nothing. Guide me through this valley, strengthen my heart, and fill me with perfect peace, for you are my light, rock, and salvation. It's in you; I am safe in your arms. Amen.

Closing Prayer and Words from the Author

I dedicate this book to survivors, caregivers, and their families. I want to encourage you not to let your circumstances defeat you. The key to an unshakeable spirit lies in one simple truth. The power to rise above your circumstances to weather any storm that comes your way lies within *You*. It's a choice you make every single day—a decision to focus on what you can control and let go of what you can't. You see, life is full of obstacles and setbacks; it's easy to get caught up in the negativity, to let the weight of your problems crust your spirit and steal your joy, but when you learn to act as if nothing bothers you by telling yourself ALL is WELL, you take back control of your life. You refuse to let external circumstances dictate your happiness. Allow my testimony to prove how God can change things in your life if only you believe, trust, and wait on Him.

Plan of Salvation

It's as easy as the ABCs: Admit, Believe, and Confess.

Admit: Acknowledge that you are a sinner and that you need salvation from your sins.

Believe: Believe that Jesus Christ died on the cross for your sins and rose again, offering forgiveness and eternal life.

Confess: Confess Jesus as your Lord and Savior, committing your life to Him and following His teachings.

Lords Prayer

Lord Jesus, come into my life, save me. I admit I am a sinner; I believe you died on the cross for my sins and rose again. I confess you are lord and Savior, and I commit my life to you. Amen

Resource Page

Effects of Stroke | Johns Hopkins Medicine

Stroke awareness: Know the causes and symptoms.

After all, strokes are more common than you might believe: There's one every 40 seconds in the United States.

How can you minimize your physical risk of having a stroke? With practical steps, such as lowering your blood pressure, watching your weight, exercising, drinking moderately, and avoiding tobacco. It's also important to recognize a stroke's symptoms. They're easier to remember if you think of the word "FAST."

- F is for facial drooping: Does one side of the face droop or feel numb?
- A is for arm weakness: When lifting both arms, does one drift downward?
- S is for speech difficulty: Is speech slurred or hard to understand?
- T is the time to call 911: If you notice any of these symptoms, seek emergency help - even if the symptoms are temporary.

Centers for Disease Control and Prevention. "Stroke facts." Accessed April 13, 2021. https://www.cdc.gov/stroke/facts.htm

https://www.stroke.org/en/about-stroke/types-of-stroke/hemorrhagic-strokes-bleeds

About the Author

Menzaire Boykins-Esters is a daughter, sister, aunt, wife, stroke survivor, encourager, and business owner who has been saved by God's grace. But those who know Menzie have often described her as soft-spoken and caring,  making a mighty impact in the lives of others.

Inspired by a quote by an unknown author, "Never look down on anyone unless you are admiring their shoes," Menzie strives to live by this standard in all aspects of her daily life.

As a stroke survivor, Menzie knows firsthand the importance of faith and its impact on one's journey. She is passionate about motivating others to prioritize their well-being, as she believes a healthy lifestyle is the most important tool for living a long, successful life.

Menzie has owned Divine Juicing since 2020. Her mission as a business owner is to inspire humanity to ingest healthy, organic, and fruitful divine juice that feeds the mind, body, and soul. Ultimately, she knows her primary mission is to promote healthy living while delivering compassion to the community.

After assessing the health rate in the African American Community, diabetes rates for black adults (16%) were all higher than the rate for white adults (11%). That's when Menzie saw a need to bring awareness to the community by hosting an annual World Stroke Day in May to spread awareness about the warning signs, symptoms, and prevention of a stroke.

Continuing her passion for promoting a healthy lifestyle that encourages energetic people to live prosperous lives, she has accepted the invitation to join the board of the Love Yourself for Life— LY4L non-profit organization.

Menzaire is currently the coordinator of the Knuckles Health Education Services Heart & Stroke Survivorship Group. The mission of the Knuckles Health Education Services Heart and Stroke Survivorship Support Group is to strengthen the lives of heart and stroke survivors, friends, family, and caregivers through education, support, fellowship, and encouragement as they navigate the road to recovery.

www.ingramcontent.com/pod-product-compliance
Lightning Source LLC
Chambersburg PA
CBHW071514120626
46550CB00006B/2217